THE LADYBIRD BOOK OF

LONDON

by
JOHN LEWESDON

with illustrations by
JOHN BERRY

Publishers: Wills & Hepworth Ltd., Loughborough

First Published 1961   ©   *Printed in England*

Trafalgar Square

Let us start our tour of London at Trafalgar Square, for there we are in the middle of everything. The Square was laid out in memory of Lord Nelson's great naval victory of 1805, and his statue stands on top of the one hundred and eighty-five foot column. You will like the four bronze lions designed by the Victorian artist Landseer.

When you have gazed up at Lord Nelson, and have seen the lions and the fountains, stand looking the same way as Lord Nelson. In front of you is Whitehall, which leads to Westminster Abbey, the Houses of Parliament and the River Thames. Half-right of you is Admiralty Arch, the entrance to the wide ceremonial drive to Buckingham Palace called The Mall.

To your right lies the West End, with its famous shops and hotels. On your left is the Strand, which leads to the City of London. That long building behind you is the National Gallery, where you can see many of the nation's most treasured pictures.

The pigeons, which walk about in the tamest manner, will be very grateful for any crumbs. They seem to consider themselves to be one of the sights of London. You can buy special pigeon food from vendors on the Square, and if you are very lucky or clever, the pigeons will perch on your hand to feed, or on your shoulder, or even on your head.

4   **Nelson's column in Trafalgar Square**

PICTORIAL
PLAN of LONDON

SCALE

0   ¼   ½   ¾   1 MILE

Railways and Stations ▬▬▬▬
Underground lines and Stations ---●---

This little book describes briefly some of the sights of London. It does not give details of dates and times when places of interest are open to the public, or the cost of admission where a charge is made; nor does it explain how to get there.

These facts can be obtained from guide-books, or by enquiring. One good place to get such information is from the Travel Enquiry Office at Piccadilly Circus Underground Station,

Series 618

Published by Ladybird Books Ltd
A Penguin Company
80 Strand, London WC2R 0RL

This facsimile edition © Ladybird Books Ltd MMXI
All rights reserved.
Printed in China
005

Whitehall

If we stroll down Whitehall we are in one of the most important streets in the world. It is the heart of the government of Great Britain, the centre of the British Commonwealth of Nations.

Once there was an enormous royal palace where Whitehall is now, Whitehall Palace. It was burned down in 1698 and only the name and one building, the Banqueting House, remain. You will see it on the left, almost opposite the two mounted horse-guards, a beautiful building with two rows of seven tall windows between pillars. It was from one of those windows that King Charles I stepped on to the scaffold to his execution in 1649.

The two mounted soldiers are troopers of the Queen's Life Guard, and everyone likes to look at them in their splendid uniforms, and at the glossy, patient horses. If you are there at eleven in the morning, or ten on Sundays, you can watch the ceremony of changing the guard.

In the middle of Whitehall stands the Cenotaph, the simple and dignified memorial to the men and women who died for their country in the two World Wars. It is here that the Queen lays a wreath on Remembrance Sunday.

On each side of Whitehall are big stone buildings; these are government offices. Lower down on the right is Downing Street, a quiet little street in which you will see a doorway marked No. 10. That is the home of the Prime Minister.

A Life Guardsman in Whitehall

Trooping the Colour

When we have finished looking at the splendid troopers on their fine horses, and perhaps taken a snapshot of them, we can walk through the courtyard and under the archway. We can *walk* under it, but only royalty and a few specially privileged persons can *drive* through it.

We come to a large parade ground, Horse Guards Parade. When Whitehall was a royal palace this was the tilt yard, where tournaments were held between knights in armour. On our left we can see the garden wall and the back of the Prime Minister's house, and on our right is the Admiralty. In front is St. James's Park, a lovely vista of green grass and fine trees.

The ceremony of Trooping the Colour is performed on Horse Guards Parade every year on the Queen's official birthday. The Queen has two birthdays, her own on April 21st, and her official birthday in June.

It is a magnificent spectacle when Her Majesty rides from Buckingham Palace at the head of her Household Cavalry to Horse Guards Parade. There the Queen inspects a battalion of the Foot Guards and watches them Troop the Colour, to the music of the massed bands. The soldiers are in full regimental dress, and the complicated and impressive ceremony is carried through with wonderful precision.

Buckingham Palace

At the end of the ceremony of Trooping the Colour the Guards march off Horse Guards Parade, led by the Queen herself. Let us go the same way, walking to the right across the parade ground and then down the Mall.

The Mall is a wide, pinkish road, between a double avenue of lime trees. St. James's Park is on one side, and Marlborough House and St. James's Palace are on the other. At the end stands Buckingham Palace, with the memorial to Queen Victoria in front. Buckingham Palace was built in 1703 for the Duke of Buckingham, but since the reign of Queen Victoria it has been the London home of the Sovereign. It was rebuilt to the design of the famous architect, John Nash, in 1825, and the front was again rebuilt in 1913.

When the Queen is in residence the Royal Standard flies from the masthead day and night. The Foot Guards usually provide the sentries and you can see them, in busbies and red tunics, or grey great-coats, standing in front of their sentry boxes, or marching up and down.

There is always a crowd between ten-thirty and eleven o'clock in the morning to watch the impressive ceremony of changing the guard in the forecourt.

Although the Palace is in the heart of London, it has a very large and lovely garden where the Royal Garden Parties are held in the summer.

Buckingham Palace

St. James's Palace

A short walk from Buckingham Palace takes us to St. James's Palace. We go back up the Mall a short way, turn to the left, and we shall see the charming, old brick palace. Here, too, guardsmen are on sentry duty, but they will not mind if we go into the courtyard.

St. James's Palace was built about four hundred and fifty years ago by King Henry VIII, on the site of an ancient hospital. When Whitehall Palace was burned down, St. James's became the London home of the King and Queen, until Queen Victoria moved to Buckingham Palace.

It is still the official Palace in some ways, because royal documents are signed *"From our Court of St. James's"*. Some members of the Royal Family live in the palace, and it will probably become the London residence of the Prince of Wales when he grows up and has a home of his own.

There are two royal chapels in the palace. The one off Ambassador's Court is part of the original building, and has a very beautiful painted ceiling.

When a new King or Queen is proclaimed, the proclamation is made from a balcony in Friary Court, by a Herald in his picturesque and colourful tabard. It is easy to dream of the past in the courtyards of St. James's Palace.

St. James's Park

It might be a good thing to have a rest, and so we will go back to the Mall and into St. James's Park. If it is a fine day we can sit down by the lake and watch the ducks and wild-fowl, and perhaps the pelicans.

London is one of the three biggest cities in the world, with a population, in 1952, of eight million, three hundred thousand people. Yet, right in the middle of this busy bustling city there are four parks, with a total of seven hundred and eighty-two acres of grass and trees. They are Hyde Park, Kensington Gardens, Green Park and St. James's Park.

When you think of the tremendous value of land in London, you will realise that these lovely open parks are a rich treasure indeed.

St. James's Park is the prettiest of them all. It lies between the Mall and Birdcage Walk—and what a jolly name for a street! It was originally made by King Henry VIII as a nursery for deer, and was re-designed by King Charles II, who loved to stroll in his park to feed the ducks, with which he stocked the lake. The Russian Ambassador gave King Charles a pair of pelicans, and there are still pelicans living on the islands in the lake.

We must go across the little suspension bridge over the lake, and look at the views as we go. If we feel like some refreshments, which might be a good idea, we can go to the "Cake House".

Westminster Abbey

If we cross the bridge and leave St. James's Park by the gate in the south-east corner, it is only a short walk to Westminster Abbey.

The first thing to do inside the Abbey is to stand by the slab of stone which covers the tomb of the Unknown Warrior and look around us, still and silent. Look up at the soaring pillars and the wonderfully carved ceiling. Look down the long nave to the altar. You will almost *feel* the sheer beauty of this wonderful church built to the glory of God.

The Abbey was founded by King Edward the Confessor, nine hundred years ago. Most of it was built by King Henry III two centuries later. The long chapel behind the altar was built by King Henry VII, five hundred years ago. The two tall towers at the west-end are more recent; they were built in 1740.

Westminster Abbey is very old and very beautiful, and it is full of history. All our Kings and Queens have been crowned there since the Norman Conquest, and many of them are buried in the Abbey. We can see their tombs.

When we walk round we must go to Poets' Corner, and the Coronation Chair. Our Kings and Queens sit on this throne to be crowned, and it dates back to the year 1300. Underneath the seat is the ancient Stone of Scone, which was once used for the coronation of the Kings of Scotland. In King Henry VII's Chapel you will see the banners of the Knights of the Bath, our second oldest Order of Chivalry, founded in 1399.

The West Front of Westminster Abbey

The Houses of Parliament

Across the road from the Abbey are the Houses of Parliament, with Big Ben, most famous of clocks, high in his three hundred and twenty foot tower. Big Ben is, of course, really the bell which strikes the hour.

The Palace of Westminster—the proper name for the Houses of Parliament—was the King's Palace for five hundred years, until King Henry VIII moved to the neighbouring Whitehall Palace.

The Palace of Westminster was burned down in 1834, and the building we now see was built in its place. One part of the ancient palace was saved, however, and that is where we will go first.

It is Westminster Hall, a glorious building with its famous 'hammer-beam' roof, made of Sussex oak. The Hall was first built by King William Rufus in 1097, and rebuilt, after a fire, by King Richard II in 1398. So it has stood for nearly six hundred years.

When Parliament is sitting, a Union Jack flies from the top of one of the towers, and at night a light shines. When Parliament is not sitting, in holiday times, we can go inside. In the House of Lords we can see the throne from which the Queen opens Parliament, a glittering state function.

In the House of Commons, which was rebuilt after being destroyed by bombing in the last war, we can see where our laws are made. You will see the Speaker's Chair at the end; the Government M.P.s sit on its right, and the Opposition on its left.

Houses of Parliament and ' Big Ben '

The Victoria Embankment

We must find time to have a good look at the Thames. Let us walk across the end of Westminster Bridge from the Houses of Parliament, and go down part of the Victoria Embankment.

The Thames can be called the 'Father of London', because London has grown from a settlement made on the banks of the river. That was two thousand years ago, when the Romans came, and there may have been a settlement before that. So as we stroll down the Embankment we must look at 'old Father Thames' with respect—this great river which has brought London into being.

Stop for a moment to look at Cleopatra's Needle, which, by the way, had nothing to do with the Egyptian queen. The pink granite obelisk was set up in Egypt some three thousand, five hundred years ago, and it was presented to Britain in 1819, brought here on a hazardous voyage and set up in 1878.

Further down we come to four ships which are permanently moored. They are H.M.S. *President*, H.M.S. *Chrysanthemum*, H.M.S. *Discovery*, and H.M.S. *Wellington*. We are allowed on board the *Discovery*, and that is an opportunity not to be missed. She was built for Polar research, and in 1901 she took Captain Scott and his party to the Antarctic. In Scott's cabin we can see relics of his gallant journey to the South Pole.

Walking back up the Embankment we can be sure of plenty to see on the river; barges and tugs, perhaps the River Police, and the water-buses. Let us take a trip in a water-bus.

A trip on the Thames

We go on board a smart motor launch, at Charing Cross Pier on the Embankment, for the trip to Tower Pier, the next stop downstream.

It may only be a short voyage, but it is packed with interest and gives us a fine view of London. Someone on the launch will probably point out the interesting places as we go along, such as the Royal Festival Hall, the Shot-tower, famous buildings old and new, and the names of the bridges we pass under.

There is one rather surprising thing about this voyage. It takes us from one city to another; from the City of Westminster to the City of London. Once London was a walled city with strong gates. The King lived outside London, at the Palace of Westminster, and another town grew up around the palace, which became the City of Westminster. Now both are joined in the great city we call London, but each still has its own local government.

When we pass under London Bridge we are in the Pool of London, one of the most famous stretches of river in the world. On one hand are ships and cranes, on the other a magnificent sight: the Tower of London and, up on its hill, St. Paul's Cathedral. Ahead of us is Tower Bridge.

We go ashore at Tower Pier, but before we leave the water-bus, look at the walled-up water entrance to the Tower, called Traitor's Gate.

The Pool of London

The Tower of London

The Tower of London is a castle, with the Thames on one side and a wide moat, now empty, on the other three. The oldest part is in the middle, the White Tower, which was built nine hundred years ago by William the Conqueror. Later Kings enlarged and strengthened the Tower, making it, at the same time, a mighty fortress, a palace and a prison.

You will soon see the Yeomen Warders, or 'Beefeaters', in their picturesque uniforms of four hundred years ago. There is so much to see in the Tower that we need plenty of time; time to look and time to dream a little about the past.

We must go to see the wonderful collection of armour in the White Tower, and the heavily guarded Crown Jewels in the Wakefield Tower. We must also visit the Bloody Tower, where it is believed the little princes were murdered, and the prisons and dungeons where kings, queens and noblemen have been imprisoned. Many of them walked out to Tower Green to be executed. On the first floor of the Beauchamp Tower the walls are covered with inscriptions and carvings made by prisoners long ago.

For centuries the Tower housed the royal menagerie. The wild animals have all gone now, but you will see the ravens, which live peaceably in the Tower where so much history, and so much tragedy, has been enacted.

Tower Hill and Tower Bridge

In the old days many people made their last journey from a dungeon in the Tower to Tower Hill, just outside, to have their heads struck off, or to be hanged. Only very distinguished people had the privilege of being executed privately inside the Tower, on the green; the rest were executed outside in public.

You will have noticed the great number of old cannons in and around the Tower. Many of them are prizes won in battle. The embankment by Tower Hill is one of the places where guns are fired in salute on special occasions, such as the Queen's birthday. Another place is Hyde Park. At Tower Hill sixty-one gun salutes are fired on great occasions amid splendid ceremonial.

Look at the two handsome memorials on Tower Hill. They are to the men of the Royal Merchant Navy who died in the two wars. We get a fine view of Tower Bridge, too, and the next thing we will do is to go and look at it.

Tower Bridge is the last one over the Thames before the sea, and it is the beginning of the great Port of London. So that ships can pass into the Pool of London, Tower Bridge can be opened. The road lifts up in two halves, like a pair of drawbridges.

The two halves weigh about a thousand tons each, and they are raised in one-and-a-half minutes by hydraulic power. Tower Bridge was opened in 1894. It is a fine sight to see the road rising upwards and to watch a ship passing underneath.

The City

A short bus ride, or an interesting walk, will take us to the Monument, in Fish Street. The Monument is a fluted column two hundred and two feet high, with a gilded device at the top representing flames. It was built in 1677 to commemorate the Great Fire of London of 1666, which began in a baker's shop exactly two hundred and two feet away, in Pudding Lane.

There are three hundred and eleven steps inside the Monument, and if you do not mind getting puffed, climb to the top; the view over London is wonderful.

Another short bus ride takes us through the busy streets of offices to the Mansion House, the official home of the Lord Mayor of London. Stand outside the Mansion House and look around you, for this is the very heart of the City.

Standing proudly on its island is the Royal Exchange, and its steps are another place from which a new Sovereign is proclaimed. Across the road is the Bank of England, a massive and, naturally enough, very safe-looking building.

This busy, bustling home of banks and offices has its roots deep in the history of old London. Once rich merchants lived here, and high-spirited young apprentices slept under the counters, and sallied forth eagerly when the cry "Out Clubs!" was raised, the cry calling the apprentices to fight. In this city a boy named Dick once began his career which ended with him being Sir Richard Whittington, thrice Lord Mayor of London.

The Royal Exchange

Guildhall

From the Mansion House let us walk down Prince's Street past the Bank of England, and turn left to Guildhall. Built five hundred years ago, Guildhall stands on the site where the City of London has been governed for a thousand years. Official banquets are held in Guildhall, with the Lord Mayor presiding.

The Lord Mayor of London guards and protects the City's ancient liberties. When the Sovereign visits the City on ceremonial occasions, he or she stops at Temple Bar, where one of the old gates once stood, and asks the Lord Mayor's permission to enter his city.

On each second Saturday in November, the newly-elected Lord Mayor rides in procession to the Law Courts, where he is received by the Lord Chief Justice as the Sovereign's representative. The Lord Mayor's Show is a great traditional event for Londoners.

The Lord Mayor's coach is a wonderful affair. It has been used since 1756, is very heavy and most elaborately decorated, and very strong horses have to be used to pull it along.

The greatest annual occasion held in Guildhall is the Lord Mayor's Banquet. The new Lord Mayor and the Sheriffs of the City of London entertain the retiring Lord Mayor, the Prime Minister, members of the Government, and many very distinguished persons. The old hall is ablaze with lights which shine on the precious silver and gold plate, on the jewels of the ladies, and on the rich robes of the Lord Mayor and City officials.

Guildhall

St. Paul's Cathedral

Cheapside takes us to St. Paul's, on Ludgate Hill: the Cathedral of the City of London and one of the most famous churches in the world. Inside, we must stand for a few moments underneath the great dome and look around us—and upwards. There is much to see, but first, pause to let us *feel* the magic of the great building.

Old St. Paul's, which stood on the same site, was destroyed in the Fire of London. The present Cathedral was designed by Sir Christopher Wren, and was finished in 1710. The most notable feature is the enormous dome. From the floor to the top of the cross on the dome is three hundred and sixty-five feet, the same as the number of days in a year.

St. Paul's contains memorials to many national heroes, among them Lord Nelson, Sir John Moore, the Duke of Wellington, General Gordon, Lord Roberts, Lord Kitchener, and in the crypt, Sir Christopher Wren.

There are steps up to the Whispering Gallery, inside the dome, where words whispered into the stone walls can be heard right round the other side. From the stone gallery outside we have a magnificent view of London. We can climb higher, to the Golden Gallery, round the top of the dome, and if you are still not satisfied, you can climb higher still, a total of seven hundred and twenty-seven steps from the bottom, to the inside of the golden ball under the great cross.

Greenwich

We have not finished with the 'sights of London' yet, but it might be a good idea to go for another trip on the Thames from Westminster Pier down the River to Greenwich. It is a delightful three-quarters-of-an-hour voyage through the Port of London, so look out for ships, British and foreign.

At Greenwich you will see the imposing front of the Royal Naval College, on the site of Greenwich Palace, which Queen Elizabeth I used so often. We can go inside the Naval College at certain times to see the Painted Hall and the Chapel.

Across the road is the exquisite Queen's House, now part of the National Maritime Museum. It is full of perfect models of ships of every period, and there are charts, nautical instruments, and the Nelson Gallery. This contains many relics of the great admiral, even the uniform he wore at the Battle of Trafalgar.

The Royal Observatory was at Greenwich from the days of King Charles II until 1950, when it was moved. But you can still see the strip of brass which marks Meridian O. If you stand astride it you can truthfully say that you are standing in both the western and the eastern hemispheres.

We must also go on board the *Cutty Sark* which is preserved at Greenwich. She is the only survivor of the famous tea clippers which used to race home from the Far East in the last century. Her glorious and graceful lines make it easy to imagine her speeding through the ocean with her great sails set.

The Cutty Sark at Greenwich

The British Museum

Back in London again let us go to the British Museum in Bloomsbury. There are three main divisions: Archaeology, the Library, and the Collection of Prints and Drawings. The Natural History Department is housed in its own Museum at South Kensington.

The great domed Reading Room of the British Museum is used by scholars, for there they can study ancient manuscripts and books not to be found elsewhere in the world.

The British Museum is so full of interest that you never have enough time to see all you want. In a short visit, there are some treasures we must be sure not to miss. We must look at the Rosetta Stone in the Egyptian Sculpture Gallery, which dates back to the year 196 B.C. It was from the writing on this stone that scholars learned how to read ancient Egyptian writing. Look also at the mummies of sacred animals, the wooden coffins and the wall paintings, some of which are three thousand, five hundred years old.

The Elgin Marbles are priceless statues from the Parthenon at Athens, built about 433 B.C. Have a look at the Roman and early British exhibits, and especially the treasures from the Anglo-Saxon burial ship from Sutton Hoo, and the Mildenhall Treasure.

In the Manuscript Saloon, we can see Magna Carta, the log book of H.M.S. *Victory* with Nelson's last entry, and Captain Scott's Antarctic diary.

The Egyptian Room in the British Museum

The Science Museum

There are many fine museums in London, but the one we will go to next is the Science Museum in South Kensington.   What an exciting place it is!

Downstairs is the Children's Gallery with models, scenes and pictures, and a very clear explanation of everything.   Among other things, you can see a model of a coal mine and a wheelwright's shop.

In the main hall there is a splendid array of engines, with such as *Puffing Billy* (1813) and the *Rocket* (1829)—the actual engines themselves!

You can examine old motor cars, motor cycles and bicycles, from the earliest days.   Everything is there at the Science Museum: telephones and radar, atomic power and sewing machines, the controls of an airliner and the bridge of a ship.   Many of the models have handles or buttons, so that you can make them work.

In its own building is the aeronautical section, with the earliest aeroplanes and the most modern, and everything to do with flying.

Near to each other, in South Kensington, are the Victoria and Albert Museum, the Geological Museum, and the Natural History Museum.   They are full of interest, with the exhibits beautifully arranged.   In the Natural History Museum you can even see the skeleton of a dinosaur, a prehistoric monster as big as a motor bus!

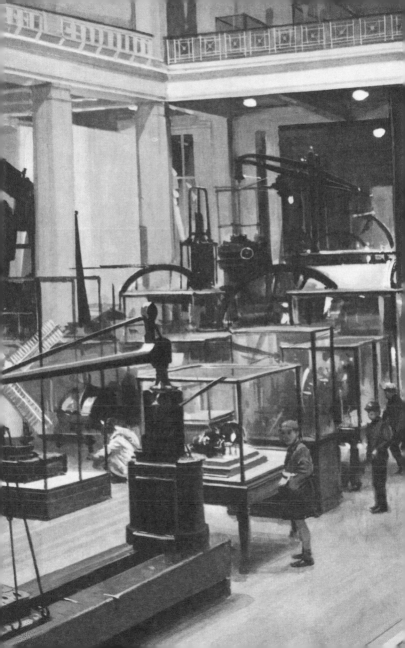

The Zoo

What could be better than a fine day at the Zoo, or the Zoological Gardens, to use the proper name? The Zoo is in Regent's Park; and we can go all the way by bus or taxi, or by underground and bus.

All the wild animals and birds are there: lions and tigers, elephants and giraffes, sea-lions and penguins, hippos and rhinos, polar bears and brown bears, parrots and monkeys. The best time to visit the animals is when they are being fed. Then we can watch the sea-lions catching their fish or diving into the water for them, and we can see the lions taking their great chunks of raw meat in their lordly way. In the wonderful monkey house we can see the monkeys scramble up trees and carefully peel their bananas.

Children can have animal rides, and who does not like riding on an elephant? An elephant will graciously take a bun or a biscuit and put it in his mouth, or take a penny and pass it to his keeper.

You go under the tunnel to visit the giraffes in their very tall house. Their necks always seem to be longer than you expected! Then go and see the hippos, and read the notice which points out that if you do not like the smell the hippos do, thank you!

In Pet's Corner, which is open during the summer, you can handle the young and tame animals. It costs extra to go to the Aquarium, but it is well worth while.

Feeding the Sea-lions

Madame Tussaud's and the Planetarium

We must be sure to visit two places, both near to Baker Street Underground station. They are Madame Tussaud's Waxworks and the Planetarium.

The waxworks have been in London since 1802, and it is a fascinating exhibition of life-size models of people. We can see famous scenes from history, such as the execution of Mary Queen of Scots; historical groups such as King Henry VIII and his wives, and well-known people of to-day. The historical groups are especially interesting because of the costumes.

You must be careful of one thing; before you ask an attendant the way, make sure he *is* an attendant and not a waxwork figure!

Next door to Madame Tussaud's is one of London's newest buildings, the Planetarium. We go into a round hall with a big dome, and sit in comfortable seats tilted backwards. The show lasts an hour. The lights go out, the dome lights up to look exactly like the night sky, and the moon, planets and stars appear. There is soft music while slowly the heavens change, as they would during the night. A voice explains the heavens, the movements of the heavenly bodies and the mysteries of space. For people who are space-minded, there is nothing like the Planetarium.

Kew Gardens

After the waxworks and our study of space, let us come down to earth and go to see the most famous gardens in the world. A pleasant bus ride, or a trip on the underground, takes us to Kew Gardens—the Royal Botanic Gardens. On a fine day it is an outing you will never forget.

Kew is much more than just a lovely park, it is a great laboratory for botanists, where plants are studied and developed by experts. It was at Kew, for example, that the special kind of wheat was developed for the vast prairies of Canada. The experts at Kew also prepared the best kind of rubber trees for Malaya and brought a great industry into being.

It is not necessary to be an expert gardener to enjoy yourself at Kew. You will get a thrill from the many interesting buildings, such as the Herbarium, where they have more than *three million* plants! There are enormous hot-houses. You can go into a very hot one to see the plants that thrive in the jungles of the Amazon in South America.

Kew Gardens began as the garden to Kew House in 1759. In those days royalty lived at Kew, and you can see the Palace, which used to be called the Dutch House, and the Queen's Cottage.

You can stroll by the Thames or the beautiful lake, and enjoy a picnic by the Chinese Pagoda. We must be sure to see the flagstaff which was made from a single spar of Douglas spruce, and stands two hundred and fourteen feet in height.

The Pagoda in Kew Gardens

Hampton Court Palace

Hampton Court is not far from Kew Gardens, and we must be sure to go there to see the great palace of mellowed red brick, which has stood on the banks of the Thames for more than four hundred years.

The Palace was begun by Cardinal Wolsey in 1515, but when he fell into disgrace, King Henry VIII took it, and it was a royal palace for two centuries. Wandering round Hampton Court, it is easy to imagine those far-off days when the courtyards, gardens, state rooms, presence chambers, galleries and the Great Hall were crowded with magnificently dressed courtiers and princes.

We enter across a fine bridge over the old moat and through the Great Gatehouse, and cross the Base Court and the Clock Court to the King's Staircase. This leads to the Guard Chamber, with a wonderful collection of arms and armour. Then we go through a long series of handsome state apartments, with old furniture, pictures and tapestries.

Downstairs we can wonder at the enormous kitchens, pantries and wine cellars. Outside you must go and see the huge vine, which is said to have been planted in 1769, and is still flourishing. We must go to the Orangery, too, and the exquisite royal gardens. And, of course, we must go to the famous maze, with six-foot-high hedges. The object is to find your way to the middle; just try if you can do it!

London Airport

London is such a very large city that its airport has to be situated a long way out. It is fourteen miles from Trafalgar Square, but there are several ways of getting there, and the journey is well worth making.

We can go into a public enclosure at the airport and watch airliners of all types arriving and taking-off, from and to every part of the world. All the while a commentary on loud-speakers tells us about every flight; the type of aircraft, its nationality, where it has come from or where it is going and, sometimes, the names of important passengers.

London Airport is one of the largest and busiest in the world, and the flow of traffic is never-ending. You will be impressed by the matter-of-fact skill with which the giant airliners are handled, taking-off or touching down at exactly the right place at the right time. The names of the far-away places are exciting; and we feel that we are at one of the busiest cross-roads in the world.

The authorities of the airport are pleased to see us, and they have arranged everything for our pleasure and interest. We can buy refreshments or a full meal. For children who are not above old-fashioned means of transport, they have pony-rides and a miniature railway. There is even a sand-pit for the very young. But the great thrill is the aeroplanes; huge and graceful, immensely powerful and so beautiful to watch.

Piccadilly Circus

London is so full of interesting places that it would take a very long time to see everything. In our tour we have seen much, but much has been left out. We have not been to the many wonderful art galleries, and there are more museums than we have mentioned. There are dozens of quaint or interesting old houses, and the beautiful City churches.

One very important feature of London, and one which foreigners always admire, is the London Policeman. Remember he is your friend; if you want any help, or if you should get lost, never hesitate, ask a policeman. He will never fail you.

You will have admired the cheerful red buses which you see everywhere, and the taxi-cabs which their drivers handle so cleverly. You will certainly have been thrilled with the Underground. This network of tunnels deep underneath London is unique. Visitors are always fascinated by the escalators, the brightly-lit stations, and the rush of the trains from the dark tunnels.

Perhaps the best place to end a visit to London is Piccadilly Circus, especially at night when the lights are blazing. This is one of the best-loved spots in London, with its little statue of Eros in the middle. For Englishmen living abroad Piccadilly Circus is the symbol of home, for it is the very heart of London.

Piccadilly Circus at Night

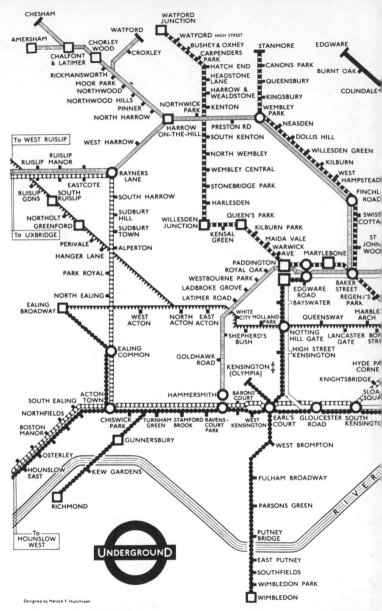

Designed by Harold F Hutchison

By Permission of London Transport.